Guerrilla Warfare Tactics
in Urban Environments

Patrick D. Marques

This is a curated and comprehensive collection of the most important works covering matters related to national security, diplomacy, defense, war, strategy, and tactics. The collection spans centuries of thought and experience, and includes the latest analysis of international threats, both conventional and asymmetric. It also includes riveting first person accounts of historic battles and wars.

Some of the books in this Series are reproductions of historical works preserved by some of the leading libraries in the world. As with any reproduction of a historical artifact, some of these books contain missing or blurred pages, poor pictures, errant marks, etc. We believe these books are essential to this collection and the study of war, and have therefore brought them back into print, despite these imperfections.

We hope you enjoy the unmatched breadth and depth of this collection, from the historical to the just-published works.

GUERRILLA WARFARE TACTICS IN URBAN ENVIRONMENTS

A thesis presented to the Faculty of the US Army
Command and General Staff College in partial
fulfillment of the requirements for the
degree

MASTER OF MILITARY ART AND SCIENCE
General Studies

by

PATRICK D. MARQUES, MAJ, USA
B.A., Indiana University, Bloomington, Indiana, 1990

Fort Leavenworth, Kansas
2003

MASTER OF MILITARY ART AND SCIENCE

THESIS APPROVAL PAGE

Name of Candidate: MAJ Patrick D. Marques

Thesis Title: Guerrilla Warfare Tactics In Urban Environments

Approved by:

_____, Thesis Committee Chairman
LTC Taylor V. Beattie, M.A.

_____, Member
James H. Willbanks, Ph.D.

_____, Member
MAJ Susan E. Mitchell, J.D.

Accepted this 6th day of June 2003 by:

_____, Director, Graduate Degree Programs
Philip J. Brookes, Ph.D.

The opinions and conclusions expressed herein are those of the student author and do not necessarily represent the views of the US Army Command and General Staff College or any other governmental agency. (References to this study should include the foregoing statement.)

ABSTRACT

GUERRILLA WARFARE TACTICS IN URBAN ENVIRONMENTS by MAJ Patrick D. Marques, 57 pages.

Current Special Forces doctrine is very limited concerning the conduct of guerrilla warfare combat operations in urban environments. The focus of the current doctrine is on conducting combat operations in rural environments. The material available on urban environments is defined in broad terms primarily focused on the larger picture of unconventional warfare. Some considerations and characteristics of urban tactical operations are addressed but are so general they could be applied to a conventional infantry unit as easily as to a guerrilla force. Traditionally, Special Forces guerrilla warfare doctrine has focused on its conduct in a rural environment as historically, most guerrilla movements have formed, operated, and been supported outside of the cities. Increasing world urbanization is driving the "center of gravity" of the resistance, the populace and their will to resist, into urban settings. As populations have gravitated to the cities on every continent, the ability to prosecute a successful guerrilla war has often depended on the ability to conduct combat operations in these environments. Predominantly, the aspects of unconventional warfare that were executed in urban settings were those such as intelligence activities, recruiting, sabotage, or subversion. Guerrilla warfare combat operations were done in urban environments only when absolutely necessary.

ACKNOWLEDGMENTS

Several people assisted me in the completion of this thesis. First and foremost were my committee members. LTC Taylor Beattie, Dr. James Willbanks, and MAJ Susan Mitchell provided a tremendous amount of advice and assistance throughout the process. Others who deserve attention are Mr. Kevin Shea, Mr. Timothy Thomas, Mr. Lester Grau, LTC Angus Fay, and many of the staff members of the Combined Arms Research Library on Fort Leavenworth.

TABLE OF CONTENTS

ACRONYMS

ASU	Active Service Units
DA	Department of the Army
DoD	Department of Defense
DRA	Democratic Republic of Afghanistan
FM	Field Manual
INLA	Irish National Liberation Army
IRA	Irish Republican Army
PIRA	Provisional Irish Republican Army
RIRA	Real Irish Republican Army
RPG	rocket propelled grenade
RUC	Royal Ulster Constabulary
TTP	tactics, techniques, and procedures
US	United States
UW	unconventional warfare

CHAPTER 1

INTRODUCTION

The topic of this thesis is "Guerrilla Warfare Tactics in Urban Environments." It examines the tactics and techniques used in combat operations by various guerrilla forces in urban environments. Although traditional guerrilla warfare has been primarily a rural endeavor, as populations have gravitated to the cities on every continent the ability to prosecute a successful guerrilla war has often depended on the ability to conduct combat operations in these environments. However, the question remains whether Special Forces doctrine has kept up with this phenomenon by addressing the employment of guerrilla forces in combat operations in urban environments. Urban guerrilla warfare is not a new idea, and has been primarily a means to support, draw attention away from, or accompany the primary guerrilla forces operating in the rural areas. As a result, the historical actions of guerrillas that were predominantly executed in urban settings, and thus addressed in Special Forces doctrine, were those such as intelligence activities, recruiting, sabotage, or subversion. No doubt these activities should continue to be utilized in this fashion in the future when applicable. Little focus has been given to guerrilla warfare combat operations in urban environments as they were conducted only when absolutely necessary due to the inherent risks of attacking military or police forces in the cities. However, the end of the twentieth century has shown a significant increase in urban guerrilla warfare combat operations throughout the world, most often as a necessary means to prosecute the war. The guerrilla survives and succeeds by his dependence upon the populace and their support of his actions. In many areas of the world, and most often in the least developed countries, the populace has increasingly moved into and around the cities as the communities have shifted from rural-based to urban-based societies (Taw 1994). The guerrilla must do the same if he is to gain their material and moral support. If the guerrillas of a US-sponsored insurgency have been forced closer to or within urban areas to accomplish their mission then Special Forces units must be prepared to organize, train, advise, assist, and employ them in the conduct of guerrilla combat operations in the cities.

This thesis will focus on guerrilla warfare combat operations (ambush, raid, and sniper operations) conducted in urban environments. Ancillary activities such as reconnaissance, collaboration with the populace, and command and control will be addressed as they pertain to the guerrillas' accomplishment of their combat operations. It will not be addressing intelligence activities, sabotage, subversion, guerrilla logistical support and/or caching, training, or basing considerations. All of these areas are certainly important aspects of a successful guerrilla war and some have significant tactics, techniques, and procedures (TTP) for urban environments already established in doctrine. Specified TTP for the employment of guerilla forces in urban combat operations is more difficult to find. Another limitation of the scope of this thesis will be the use of only certain historical examples. This thesis will research the tactics of the Irish Republican Army (IRA) from 1969 to the present, the Afghan Mujahideen during the Soviet occupation on Afghanistan from 1979 to 1989, and Chechen rebels during the Battles for Grozny in 1994 and 2000. These case studies were chosen for their relatively modern time frames, which allowed for more availability of resources detailing the tactics used, and their particularly different aspects of urban guerrilla warfare. The IRA operate in essentially peacetime conditions and almost completely covertly, rarely taking up direct combat with the British military or security forces. The Mujahideen lived and operated primarily in rural areas, and moved into the cities to conduct specific combat operations as their needs called for. The Chechens lived, operated, and fought within Grozny and were in near constant violent contact with the Russians.

The primary question that will be answered by this thesis is Does the current Special Forces doctrine for guerrilla warfare combat operations TTP need modifications or additions for application in urban environments? Several secondary questions must then be addressed. What historical examples of guerrilla warfare have significant urban combat activities? How is the effectiveness of urban guerrilla warfare combat operations TTP measured? What legal considerations would prevent US Special Forces from using some of the tactics researched? Tertiary questions that will follow include: What are the current guerrilla warfare combat operations TTP found in Special Forces doctrine? What urban combat operations TTP were used in the researched historical examples? Were they successful? How did they differ from established TTP for guerrilla combat operations in current Special Forces doctrine? Should they be included in Special Forces doctrine for guerrilla warfare? Why? These secondary and tertiary questions support the primary question by establishing what is documented now, what others have done before, and what made them successful or unsuccessful.

This thesis assumed the historical references used were factual and accurate. To ensure this, as many different references as possible of the same historical example were used and any examples with significant factual differences between references were discarded.

3

This thesis uses several key terms throughout. The primary terms used are unconventional warfare, urban areas, combat operations, insurgency, and guerrilla warfare. Unconventional warfare (UW) is defined as "a broad spectrum of military and paramilitary operations, predominately conducted through, with, or by indigenous or surrogate forces organized, trained, equipped, supported, and directed in varying degrees by an external source. UW includes, but is not limited to, guerrilla warfare, subversion, sabotage, intelligence activities, and unconventional assisted recovery" (DA 2001a, 2-1). Urban area is defined as "a concentration of structures, facilities, and people that form the economic and cultural focus for the surrounding area" (DA 2002a, 1-2). Combat operations are defined as the offensive actions of raid, ambush, and sniper activities in which guerrilla forces use direct and indirect fire to engage enemy forces. An insurgency is "an organized movement aimed at the overthrow of a constituted government through use of subversion and armed conflict" (DoD 2001, 215). Guerrilla warfare is defined as "military and paramilitary operations conducted by irregular, predominately indigenous forces against superior forces in enemy-held or hostile territory. It is the overt military aspect of an insurgency" (DA 2001b, 1-1). A resistance organization of an insurgency is usually composed of three elements: the guerrilla force, the auxiliary, and the underground. This thesis will focus on the operations of the guerrilla force, the overt military or paramilitary arm of the insurgency. The auxiliary, which supplies and supports the insurgency, and the underground, which conducts the above mentioned sabotage, subversion, and intelligence gathering activities, will be addressed only in their direct support of guerrilla combat operations. Subversion and sabotage must also be defined because the two activities are so often linked to insurgencies in general they are

4

incorrectly thought to fall under the heading of guerrilla warfare. Subversion and sabotage, combined with guerrilla warfare and other activities, are aspects of the Unconventional Warfare mission, as defined above. Subversion "undermines the political, military, economic, or psychological strength of a nation or occupying power. Subversion attacks the internal or international legitimacy of targeted governments or powers and their actions" (DA 2001a, 2-8). Sabotage "injures or obstructs the national defense of a nation by willfully damaging or destroying any national defense or war material, premises, or utilities, including human and natural resources" (DA 2001a, 2-9). These two activities are predominately carried out by the underground arm of an insurgency and not the guerrilla force. The terms "urban guerrilla warfare" and "terrorism" are often used interchangeably. To ensure a delineation between the two, terrorism is defined as "the calculated use of unlawful violence or threat of unlawful violence to inculcate fear; intended to coerce or to intimidate governments or societies in the pursuit of goals that are generally political, religious, or ideological" (DoD 2001, 437).

Two predominant problems were associated with the research and compilation of this thesis. The first was gaining accurate accounts and descriptions of the actual tactics used by guerrilla forces in their urban combat operations. The second was determining the literal success and usefulness of those tactics.

The first problem required getting past the broad analysis of what the researched combat operations did and discovering how they executed the operations to the greatest detail possible. This involved background reading concerning the general topic of urban guerrilla warfare. Guerrilla warfare is a popular subject for authors, either in general or concerning a specific case. Most focus on "what" the guerrillas did, and "why" they did it. Few get into the details of "how" they conducted their operations. Additionally, the case studies examined did not have direct US involvement. The Foreign Military Studies Office (FMSO) has produced several works concerning the Afghan and Chechen case studies and the primary authors were available for further research and direction to alternate sources of information. To bridge this gap between broad analysis and actual tactics with the IRA case study, interviews were conducted with British officers who have served multiple tours in Northern Ireland.

The second problem required establishing the conditions in which the combat operations were done and what aspects of those conditions were critical to their success. To determine the success or failure of various TTP used in urban guerrilla warfare combat operations requires an understanding of the overall goals and objectives of the particular insurgents being studied. The context of the actions taken must be considered in order to formulate and evaluate measures of effective urban guerrilla combat operations. This involved establishing specific criteria by which to measure the effectiveness of the TTP used in the researched combat operations. The criteria must span three subjects in order to evaluate the current Special Forces TTP for guerrilla combat operations and the TTP used in the historical examples. The first area that must be applied to the criteria is that of urban operations characteristics. "Collateral damage to local populace or facilities" would be an example of this criterion. The second subject area includes the principles of guerrilla warfare, such as "security." The final subject area is that of legal considerations. Urban guerrillas have often employed significant unconventional tactics in order to surprise and deceive enemy forces. Some of these tactics tread a thin line between legal and illegal actions when applied against US

national and international laws. An example is the use of civilian noncombatants for

deception operations. Each criterion will be defined and further broken down into more

detailed aspects for evaluation.

CHAPTER 2

LITERATURE REVIEW

Existing literature on guerrilla warfare is extensive and the material dedicated specifically to urban guerrilla warfare is significant. This chapter will focus the review of available literature into the three subjects of US Army Special Forces doctrine and field manuals, general literature on the subject of urban guerrilla warfare, and resources specific to the case studies researched.

Special Forces Doctrine

Current Army Special Operations Forces and Special Forces doctrine consists of two primary manuals, FM 100-25, *Doctrine For Army Special Operations Forces*, and FM 3-05.20, *Special Forces Operations*. As the doctrinal foundation for subordinate Army Special Operations Forces doctrine, FM 100-25 describes the principles, fundamentals, guidelines, and conceptual framework to facilitate interoperability with both conventional forces and other Services' special operations forces (DA, 1999). Due to its nature the manual addresses only broad concepts of the missions of Special Forces and their employment considerations. As a result, the urban aspect of Unconventional Warfare, and more specifically guerrilla warfare, is not addressed. FM 3-05.20, the keystone manual for Special Forces operations, describes its roles, missions, capabilities, organization, command and control, employment, and sustainment operations across the operational continuum (DA, 2001a). The importance of addressing the impact of urban environments on Special Forces missions is noted in several areas of the manual.

8

Specifically, it emphasizes the affects global urbanization has on the contemporary unconventional warfare environme nt and its relevancy to Special Forces operations:

> Global urbanization is another environmental factor impacting Unconventional Warfare operations. Urbanization dictates a shift in Special Forces emphasis from rural Unconventional Warfare to all aspects of overt, low-visibility, covert, and clandestine Unconventional Warfare operations. The urbanized strategic environment provides a fertile environment for Unconventional Warfare. The battleground where Unconventional Warfare will be conducted is no longer just the inaccessible terrain of rural areas. It is also located within the increasing urban sprawl occurring worldwide. Urbanization may require the development of new skills and core competencies. (DA 2001a, 2-10)

FM 3-05.20 focuses on the operational level of Special Forces operations and any TTP for the conduct of guerrilla warfare in urban environments must be found elsewhere.

FM 3-05.201, *Special Forces Unconventional Warfare Operations*, currently in its initial draft, will form the doctrinal basis for unconventional warfare missions and will provide TTP for their conduct. In its current draft form the manual recognizes the emergence of global urbanization and that this may require a shift in emphasis from the rural to the urban guerrilla. An appendix within FM 3-05.201 (initial draft) is dedicated to unconventional warfare in urban environments. The appendix addresses the generalities of urban unconventional warfare, focusing on some historical vignettes that describe why some insurgencies transition to urban areas, general characteristics of cities, and broad tactical considerations for operations in urban environments. TTP for the employment of guerrilla forces in urban areas is not included. A lengthy chapter on the employment of resistance forces includes TTP for conducting raids, ambushes, and air defense operations in rural environments but does not include considerations or techniques for similar combat operations in urban areas.

Past Special Forces doctrine has also focused primarily on the employment of guerrilla forces in rural environments. Doctrinal manuals from the 1950s, focused on the Cold War unconventional warfare scenario of conducting guerrilla warfare in Eastern Europe, hardly address the urban environment. The 1969 version of FM 31-21, *Special Forces Operations*, begins the doctrinal recognition that urban guerrilla warfare is a viable endeavor and can be conducted not only by the underground element of a resistance but also by the guerrilla force. The rising importance of urban guerrilla operations is seen also by the fact that this manual addresses it under its chapter on counter-insurgency. Up to this point any mention of urban guerrilla operations is general at best with no TTP offered, but this changes with the 1988 TC 31-29, *Special Forces Operational Techniques* manual. The entire chapter, "Combat Operations in an Urban Environment," is dedicated to urban TTP. Unfortunately, it is essentially urban combat soldier skills such as moving past a window, crossing open areas, and entering a building. The TTPs are verbatim out of the same time period's FM 90-10-1, *An Infantryman's Guide to Combat in Built-Up Areas*. No TTP for the employment of guerrilla forces in urban combat operations are given. The 1990 version of FM 31-20, *Doctrine for Special Forces Operations*, also recognizes the possibility of urban-based guerrilla warfare. It cites the modern insurgencies of the Tupamaros in Uruguay and the Monteneros in Argentina, both almost exclusive urban insurgencies, as examples that the classic rural insurgency may no longer be the norm for contemporary political violence.

General Urban Guerrilla Warfare Literature

Trends in research of urban guerrilla warfare focus on theory and organization, what drives the guerrillas to urbanize their actions, and how urban guerrilla warfare can be countered. This background reading concerning the general topic of urban guerrilla warfare permits a solid understanding of the aspects and characteristics of urban guerrilla warfare but rarely goes into any detail on how the guerrillas conducted their operations. A common theme is global urbanization and the growing normalcy of urban insurgencies. Many works, such as *The Urbanization of Insurgency*, by Jennifer M. Taw and Bruce Hoffman, document the rise of urban insurgencies in conjunction with increasing global urbanization over the last thirty years and analyze the reasons for their success or failure. Several books on the subject also seem to use the terms urban guerrilla warfare, terrorism, and sabotage almost interchangeably, delineating no difference in these actions.

Often there are pieces of information used throughout the source that can be tied together to get a clear picture of tactical application. One such example is Jay Mallin's *Terror and Urban Guerrillas: A Study of Tactics and Documents*. A compilation of short works on the topic of urban guerrilla warfare, Mallin's book spans from a strategic and theoretical paper entitled "Partisan Warfare" by Vladimir Lenin to an operational handbook by Carlos Marighella, *The Minimanual of the Urban Guerrilla*. Marighella's manual itself begins with theoretical and political elements but eventually moves into the tactical realm of urban guerrilla warfare, encompassing everything from an urban guerrilla's marksmanship skills to the conduct of raids and ambushes.

Of particular interest is a paper written by MAJ William H. Ferrell III, USMC Judge Advocate officer, entitled *No Shirt; No Shoes; No Status: Uniforms, Distinction, and Special Operations in International Armed Conflict*. MAJ Ferrell, through the use of a hypothetical situation involving Special Operations Forces, examines the legal use of civilian and non-standard uniforms by US forces during combat operations. This and other legal issues can have a tremendous impact on the combat employment of guerrillas in urban environments by US Special Forces.

Case-Study Specific Literature

The Irish Republican Army (1969-Present)

Literature on IRA urban combat tactics is difficult to find. Most of the material focuses on broad strategic or operational themes or covers the historical and chronological aspects of the conflict. The *Handbook for Volunteers of the Irish Republican Army: Notes on Guerrilla Warfare*, issued by their General Headquarters in 1956, is a manual covering historic Irish guerrillas, general principles and strategies, and guerrilla warfare tactics. The work is very detailed at times, even describing explosive charge calculations and how to plan for combat operations. However, it is completely focused on rural operations and as its printing date indicates, it was developed prior to the start of significant urban actions by the IRA which really began in 1969. Mr. J. Bowyer Bell's book, *IRA Tactics and Targets*, although slim on methods and techniques of combat operations, is very informative concerning the types and reasoning for the targets of IRA actions over the years.

The Marine Corps Intelligence Activity published the *Urban Warfare Study: City Case Studies Compilation*, a publication that examines the Russian experiences in Chechnya, Israeli experiences in urbanized southern Lebanon, and British military experiences in Northern Ireland. Although each case study is focused on analyzing the lessons learned by the conventional force in question, tactical concerns over methods and techniques of the guerrillas are addressed.

12

Interviews were conducted with two British officers, each with multiple tours in Northern Ireland, than span a timeframe from the early 1980s to the late 1990s. These interviews proved invaluable in describing the IRA's TTPs from a first-person account. Not only were these officers able to recount their personal experiences but also the historical IRA tactics they necessarily had to study in order to be prepared for operations in Northern Ireland.

The Mujahideen in Soviet-Occupied Afghanistan (1979-1989)

The Soviet-Afghan war of the 1980s has produced significantly more detailed research of the tactics used by both the Soviets and the Mujahideen. Foremost in this research is that produced by Mr. Lester Grau of the Foreign Military Studies Office at Fort Leavenworth, Kansas. *The Bear Went Over the Mountain: Soviet Combat Tactics in Afghanistan* is a compilation of forty-seven vignettes of combat actions in Afghanistan that was originally constructed by the Frunze Combined Arms Academy in Moscow which Mr. Grau has translated and added some editorial notes for clarifications and analysis. Primarily focused on the Soviet tactics used in battles and engagements outside of the cities, certain vignettes do cover limited urban engagements in villages and towns. In conjunction with Ali Ahmed Jalali, a former Afghan Army Colonel and later a member of the Mujahideen, Mr. Grau wrote *The Other Side of the Mountain: Mujahideen Tactics in the Soviet-Afghan War*. This book is also a compilation of vignettes gained through interviews conducted in Pakistan and Afghanistan with Mujahideen fighters. Certainly an authoritative work on the topic, *The Other Side of the Mountain* describes in detail the tactics used by the guerrilla forces during the war. Most importantly, an entire chapter is dedicated specifically to urban guerrilla combat and how the Mujahideen conducted these operations in cities throughout the country.

Russian-Soviet Unconventional Wars in the Caucasus, Central Asia, and Afghanistan, a Leavenworth Paper written by Dr. Robert F. Baumann, analyzes the Russian, and later Soviet, military experiences in the Central Asian region from the late 1700s through the Soviet-Afghan war of the 1980s. Primarily focused on strategic and operational levels of the case-study conflict it often cites the use of urban guerrilla warfare by the Mujahideen and its effects on the Soviet military operations.

Another key work is *The Soviet-Afghan War: How a Superpower Fought and Lost*, translated and edited by Mr. Lester Grau and Michael A. Gress. It is a comprehensive study by the Russian General Staff that covers all aspects of the Soviet military experience in the war to include combat support and combat service support operations. Mujahideen tactics, both rural and urban, are addressed throughout.

The Chechen Rebels in the Battles for Grozny (1994 and 2000)

As with the previous case study, much of the detailed research conducted on the urban guerrilla warfare tactics of the Chechen rebels has come out of the Foreign Military Studies Office. Mr. Timothy Thomas has extensively researched both battles of Grozny and has interviewed many of the participants on the Russian side. His primary works, *The Caucus Conflict and Russian Security: The Russian Armed Forces Confront Chechnya, Parts One, Two, and Three*, and *The Battle of Grozny: Deadly Classroom for Urban Combat*, both focused on the 1994 battle, and *Grozny 2000: Urban Combat Lessons Learned*, analyze each battle and the Russian lessons learned gained from them. All three works outline the Chechen tactics and the Russians ability to adapt to them. Several other works on the battles for Grozny are also available from the Foreign Military Studies Office that range from logistical lessons learned to the debilitating effect of disease among Russian troops during the conflicts.

RAND Arroyo Center has published *The City's Many Faces* and *Capital Preservation*, compilations of briefings and reports from the Urban Operations Conferences held in 1999 and 2000, respectively. Key works in *Capital Preservation* include *The Chechen Operation from the Viewpoint of the Military Command*, by General Anatoly Sergeevich Kulikov from the Russian Ministry of Internal Affairs and offers a first person account of the planning and execution of the 1994 Battle of Grozny primarily from an operational level. In his analysis of Russian lessons learned there is some discussion of the tactics used by the Chechens. The other key work is *Chechnya: Urban Warfare Lessons Learned* by Arthur L. Speyer, III of the Marine Corps Intelligence Activity. This work contains some very detailed information on Chechen urban tactics to include schematic diagrams of ambush formations within Grozny. *The City's Many Faces* contains two of the many works by Mr. Thomas and Mr. Grau concerning operations in Chechnya. RAND Arroyo has also published *Russia's Chechen Wars 1994-2000: Lessons from Urban Combat* by Olga Oliker. This work analyzes the strategy and tactics from both sides of the conflict and the changes each took to their approach to urban combat between the 1994 and 2000 battles.

The Marine Corps Intelligence Activity study discussed in the IRA section, the *Urban Warfare Study: City Case Studies Compilation*, examines the Russian experiences in Chechnya at the strategic, operational, and tactical levels. Chechen tactics and the Russian countermeasures are well documented in this study.

Each of the three subject areas reviewed possesses their own underlying patterns. Special Forces doctrine does provide TTP for conducting guerrilla warfare combat operations, but it is almost entirely focused on the rural environment. The general urban guerrilla warfare literature has a tendency to cover strategic or operational level concepts with little emphasis on how the guerrillas conducted their combat operations in the cities. The resources covering the specific case studies in Afghanistan and Chechnya focus on the lessons learned from the conventional force side, but in doing so provide significant insight to the tactics used by the guerrilla forces in the urban environments. The material on the IRA is generally broad, but interviews with participants have given primary source data to the research.

CHAPTER 3

RESEARCH METHODOLOGY

To determine the success or failure of various TTP used in urban guerrilla warfare combat operations requires an understanding of the overall goals and objectives of the particular insurgents being studied. The context of the actions taken must be considered in order to formulate and evaluate measures of effective urban guerrilla combat operations. This involves establishing specific criteria by which to measure the effectiveness of the TTP used in the researched combat operations. This chapter will outline the subject case studies and the criteria and methodology I used to evaluate the actions of the guerrillas.

The three case studies, although all examples of guerrilla warfare in urban areas, were chosen for their significant differences. FM 3-06.11, *Combined Arms Operations in Urban Terrain*, outlines the three conditions of urban operations that span the full spectrum of offense, defense, stability, and support. Although these conditions are meant to convey the three general aspects a conventional force would encounter in urban surroundings, they are just as applicable to the conduct of guerrilla warfare. The first condition, Urban Operations Under Surgical Conditions, is considered the least destructive and is comprised of special-purpose raids, small precision strikes, or small-scale personnel seizures (DA, 2002a). This is the condition the IRA operates from most often, where day-to-day business and life go on in the urban area in a close to permissive environment. The second condition, Urban Operations Under Precision Conditions, is essentially a semi-permissive environment in which the threat is thoroughly mixed with noncombatants. Although combat actions are involved, it is of a restrictive nature due to political or other reasons (DA, 2002a). Most stability and support operations conducted by US forces have started under this condition. The Mujahideen operated against the Soviets in the Afghan cities within these conditions. Life in the cities, although affected by the Soviet occupation, still maintained a modicum of normalcy, but large numbers of Soviet forces were present and security conditions were heightened. Lastly, Urban Operations Under High-Intensity Conditions, is the condition most often thought of when discussing military operations on urban terrain. It involves combat actions against enemy forces occupying prepared positions or conducting planned attacks on built up areas (DA, 2002a). The Chechan defense of Grozny in 1994 and 2000 are perfect examples of this condition of urban operations, which is characterized by seizing, clearing, or defending urban terrain and defeating the enemy using whatever force is necessary. These case studies span all three conditions of urban operations and offer a unique perspective on the TTP that were necessary to conduct urban guerrilla warfare in each situation.

Criteria

The criteria are taken from three broad subject areas in order to encompass the TTP used in urban guerrilla warfare combat operations. Some criteria are taken from the fundamental characteristics of urban combat operations as outlined in US Army doctrine, in order to examine if and how well the guerrillas modified their tactics to the urban environment in which they were fighting. The second subject area includes the principles of guerrilla warfare, as outlined by US Special Forces doctrine, which are considered critical to the successful employment of guerrillas in combat operations. The final subject area is that of legal considerations as particular Law of War issues become increasingly

18

important in urban areas. Each criterion will be defined and further broken down into more detailed aspects for evaluation.

The following criteria were extracted from the characteristics of urban operations as laid out of FM 3-06.11, *Combined Arms Operations in Urban Terrain*:

Small Unit Battles--Combat in urban areas, even under high-intensity conditions with large formations, is a series of small unit battles (DA, 2002a). Success is determined by individual and unit initiative, command and control, unity of effort, and training. This criterion examines the tactics used by the guerrillas when in direct contact with their enemy forces in urban conditions.

Limited Mounted Maneuver Space--Buildings, street width, rubble, debris, and noncombatants all contribute to limited mounted maneuver space inside urban areas. Armored vehicles rarely are able to operate inside urban areas without Infantry support (DA, 2002a). One of the greatest disadvantages of the guerrilla is his lack of vehicular and armor support to counter his enemy's mobility and armored combat power. The weapons and tactics used by the urban guerrillas are examined here.

Three-Dimensional Terrain--Combat in urban areas can occur on the surface, above the surface, and below the surface, as well as inside and outside of buildings (DA, 2002a). The techniques and ability of the guerrillas to capitalize on the advantages and counter the disadvantages of this complex battlespace are examined here.

Collateral Damage--Significant collateral damage can occur during combat in urban environments. This can be noncombatant collateral damage as well as structural or environmental, and can have an adverse effect on the population's support of the guerrillas (DA, 2002a). This criterion investigates whether the guerrillas planned for or

19

attempted to limit the effects of their operations and ascertains whether certain tactics inadvertently cause collateral damage by their use.

Snipers--The utility of snipers in urban combat is well documented throughout the spectrum of conflict from low intensity conflicts to total war. The use of precision long and short range fires can have a devastating effect on an enemy's morale and initiative (DA, 2002a). This criterion examines sniper employment techniques and their overall contribution to the combat operations.

Additional criteria from the principles of guerrilla warfare from FM 3-05.201, *Special Forces Unconventional Warfare Operations* (Initial Draft):

Surprise--Attacking the enemy when least expected is critical to successful guerrilla combat operations (DA, 2001b). This requires rapid force concentration, operations during limited visibility, hasty reorganization after an engagement, and a prompt withdrawal to avoid unwanted contact. It can also involve deception operations. The urban environment can be advantageous to gaining surprise through the increased cover and concealment and three-dimensional terrain. It can also put a guerrilla at a disadvantage due to the often increased number of enemy forces necessary to secure built-up areas and the decreased avenues of egress available.

Security--Preservation of forces is of paramount importance to the guerrillas (DA, 2001b). Guerrillas must constantly focus on maintaining security, both in safe haven areas and during operations, to ensure the survivability of their most critical resource, the guerrilla fighter. The ability to isolate the objective area is critical for the guerrillas to alleviate the enemy's superior numbers and armaments. As distances between enemy units in contact and possible reinforcement are generally quite less in urban areas, guerrillas must be prepared to close off their objectives to maintain surprise and mobility.

Collaboration with the Local Populace--The support of the population is the center of gravity for any successful insurgent movement (DA, 2001b). The population provides the guerrillas with recruits, information, supplies, safe havens, and sometimes even medical attention. Critical to guerrillas is the human intelligence supplied by the populace. Guerrilla forces rarely have sophisticated intelligence gathering technology and must rely almost completely on human intelligence. The urban environment can provide both advantages and disadvantages for the collection of tactical intelligence for guerrilla combat operations. The sheer density of urban environment populations and the proximity of enemy forces can hinder the guerrillas contact with civilian supporters. The fear of civilian enemy collaborators and oppressive population control measures can also separate the guerrillas from their popular support, reducing their effectiveness.

Legal considerations used as criteria:

Law of War--Two specific principles under the Law of War have an increased relevance to urban guerrilla warfare. The Principle of Military Necessity states that attacks may be made only against valid military targets and also outlines protected persons and places (US Army, 2002). Urban environments inherently provide targets of opportunity that, although not necessarily military in nature, can weaken the enemy. The Principle of Discrimination or Distinction requires that combatants be distinguished from noncombatants, and military objectives must be distinguished from protected property or protected places (US Army, 2002). More specifically, the Geneva Conventions established four conditions that must be met for guerrillas or irregular groups to be considered lawful combatants. The guerrillas would have to act under the command of a person responsible for subordinates, wear a fixed, distinctive sign, carry arms openly, and generally operate in accordance with the laws of war. Protocol I to the Geneva Conventions modified these requirements slightly. The requirement to wear a fixed, recognizable sign, such as a uniform or distinctive headgear was removed. The condition to carry arms openly was further defined to apply during each military engagement and when visible to an adversary while deploying for an attack. Finally, the requirement to operate in accordance with the laws of war was expanded in that the guerrillas must be subject to an internal disciplinary system that enforces law of war compliance (US Army, 2002). Tactics used by guerrillas that are in violation of the Law of War are not acceptable for US forces because our forces are legally bound to comply with the international laws and US legitimacy in supporting the guerrillas would be in jeopardy if those laws were violated. This criteria examines how the different guerrilla organizations operated in light of these legal considerations and if or how it affected there tactics and methods.

Using a Descriptive Methodology, observations are made of what urban guerrilla warfare TTP were used by the case study groups. The data was collected through some primary means such as interviews with participants, but was generally gained from secondary sources through previously published literature. Each case study was reviewed against the above mentioned criteria to examine if the particular criterion was addressed and the effects of its use or non-use. Most importantly, the methods used by guerrillas are examined for later analysis. The TTP used by the guerrillas in the case studies are compared to current SF doctrine. This will reveal what, if anything, is missing.

CHAPTER 4

ANALYSIS

The purpose of this chapter is essentially to answer the tertiary questions established in chapter 1. These questions asked what urban combat operations TTP were used by the guerrillas in the case studies, which of these TTP were successful for the guerrillas in question, what the current TTP for urban guerrilla warfare in Special Forces doctrine are, and if or how the case studies' TTPs differ from established TTP for guerrilla combat operations in current Special Forces doctrine. Following the criteria described in chapter 3 each case study was analyzed for how the guerrillas conducted their combat operations in urban environments and if that TTP would be beneficial to current Special Forces doctrine.

The descriptive methodology illustrates the methods and techniques of the researched guerrilla organizations. The criteria used, taken from US doctrinal characteristics of urban environments, guerrilla warfare, and relevant legal aspects of war, focused the vast amounts of information available into urban guerrilla TTPs.

The IRA

In the current campaign the whole strategy in the years 1969-1971 was to lure the British Army into a real war with the IRA, the nationalist defenders. So first and foremost and always, the military forces of Britain remain the prime target. At home, at play, out of uniform, in retirement, shopping or commuting, any member of the British army remains at risk; for the IRA seeks the man or woman, not the uniform. (Bell 1990, 29)

Different paramilitary factions have evolved over the years in Northern Ireland, such as the Provisional Irish Republican Army (PIRA), the Irish National Liberation

Army (INLA), the Real Irish Republican Army (RIRA), and others, either through an evolutionary process or ideological splits with the original IRA as it existed prior to 1969. For simplicity, the term "IRA" will be used to describe the body that has executed guerrilla combat operations against British military and Royal Ulster Constabulary (RUC) forces since 1969.

The most common urban combat operations employed by the IRA are sniping, bomb ambushes (usually command detonated), mortar attacks, and RPG attacks (Fay 2003). Raids are rare. There was a period of time in the early 1980s when the IRA attempted some raids on RUC stations and British military outposts, sometimes using homemade armored vehicles designed to penetrate the outer defenses of the outpost (Fay 2003). These raids were rarely successful primarily due to either the security apparatus around the target or a loss of operational security on the part of the IRA when planning a large operation that involved a greater number of personnel to execute than normal (Fay 2003). Essentially, raids involve too much risk because of the direct engagement necessary with the security forces (British Company Commander 2003).

Mortar attacks are a common means of attacking British and RUC patrols. Many varieties of homemade mortars have been developed by the IRA over the years (Marine Corps Intelligence Activity 1999). They are often mounted in vans with their roofs cut out, positioned within range of their target, and then remotely detonated. Small arms and explosives have been the mainstay of IRA weapons since the beginning because they are easier to procure, train on, and transport (Marine Corps Intelligence Activity 1999).

IRA combat actions are conducted by active service units (ASU), usually composed of four persons who most often know each other, but who have no natural

24

connection (i.e., not related, do not work together, are not neighbors, etc.). Although the IRA's General Headquarters issues broad guidance on operations and will sometimes designate and plan specific high-value targets, it is the local commander and ASUs who plan and execute the majority of IRA operations (Bell 1990). The ASU is very decentralized and the members may actually be in contact for only the few minutes of the action they are conducting. Their movements to the objective, equipment pick up, movement from the target, and equipment drop off is all conducted individually (British Company Commander 2003).

Bomb ambushes follow a common pattern. The first step is to create what the British call a "come-on," basically a ruse or bait of some sort to get the soldiers to come into the kill zone. This could be a civil disturbance of some kind or even a small device that appears to be a bomb (British Company Commander 2003). Once the soldiers or RUC responding get to the designated area the guerrilla detonating the bomb waits to initiate until a predetermined amount of personnel or vehicles enter the kill zone. He often has some type of mark on a wall or feature of the street that designates where the majority of targets should be in order to initiate the explosive (Fay 2003). Finally, the guerrilla would detonate the device, which depending on the size and composition of the intended targets, could vary in size from a small canister to a vehicle packed with shrapnel. Fertilizer bombs are the most common, initiated with SEMTEX (Fay 2003).

The limited mounted maneuver space of the urban environment is certainly utilized by the IRA but not to the same degree as the guerrilla movements in the other case studies. This is primarily due to the fact that the IRA did not normally contend with large numbers of armored vehicles. The IRA would occasionally target the civilian vehicles used by the British military for general transport and logistics activity (Fay 2003). They would block the front and back with other vehicles and simply walk up and shoot those inside. This tactic was not used very long because it exposed the perpetrators for later identification (Fay 2003).

The three-dimensional terrain of the urban environment, with its multistoried buildings, rows of housing units, and small streets and alleyways, is used by the IRA in a passive sense in that it makes British operations more difficult. British communications, reconnaissance, maneuver, and organized pursuit are all degraded in urban areas. Most actions by the IRA are conducted on the surface and street level because a very rapid withdrawal is necessary to avoid direct contact and capture. The IRA used underground firing ranges in the rural areas but there is no specific use of subsurface areas in the urban environments aside from burial caches of explosives, weapons, and other equipment (Fay 2003). Buildings above the street level are primarily used for observation and occasionally for sniping, but the nature of the conflict, essentially permissive with much civilian activity, makes prolonged engagements and rapid withdrawals from roofs or upper floors of buildings problematic (British Company Commander 2003).

The possibility and effects of collateral damage are very often involved in the planning of IRA operations. Some bombs were planned to go off around the maximum number of civilians, primarily for the psychological effect of showing what they were capable of doing (Bell 1990). The IRA give warnings to the media for civilian infrastructure bombs but the timeframe between the warning and the bombing would often be very short (British Company Commander 2003). This allowed the IRA to moralize themselves in later propaganda by attesting that they had given a warning of the

26

bombing (Fay 2003). Many innocent bystanders as well as security forces have been maimed or killed by IRA bombings. Sometimes this was due to mistakes such as premature detonations or warnings given too late, but at times the risk of noncombatant casualties was considered acceptable because of the importance of the target (Bell 1990). The political effects to the IRA could often be damaging when a bombing killed or injured civilians. One example is a bombing in Omagh on a Saturday morning on a busy street of the town that caused several civilian casualties. The IRA lost much legitimacy and was forced to place the blame on a splinter group to lessen the damage to themselves (Fay 2003).

Snipers are often employed in the come-on role to bait British and RUC forces into a bomb ambush. Sniper specific ASUs would be comprised of a shooter, two watchers to maintain security and observation, and one person to move the weapon after the shots were fired. At times, even children were used in the role of "weapon-mover." This meant that the sniper himself only had physical possession of the weapon for about twenty minutes (Fay 2003). When employed as the primary method of engagement, the sniper would take one or two shots then withdraw (Fay 2003). When used in the come-on role to bait security forces, it was actually better not to hit their target. An injured or killed soldier or policeman meant the patrol would be occupied with the casualty and unable to attempt pursuit and continue on into the real engagement area or kill zone (British Company Commander 2003).

The highly decentralized structure of the IRA, with local commanders and ASUs deciding upon and executing operations themselves, lends greatly to their ability to surprise British military and RUC units. Gaining intelligence and prior warning on small

27

unit, independent action by the guerrillas is almost impossible. Some reports describe the use of "front" organizations, like the Falls Taxi Association in Belfast which the IRA uses both for the support of operations and as a source of income (Baldy 1987). The "black taxis" are considered a kind of Catholic Mafia by the British who occasionally support the IRA with transportation to and from objectives (Fay 2003). A more common use of the taxis is the transportation of weapons and equipment (British Company Commander 2003). The IRA very rarely concentrates its forces for urban operations as this would decrease their element of surprise in the bustling streets of Belfast or Londonderry. Rather, all combat operations are conducted by small, highly mobile teams (Fay 2003).

Security for IRA guerrillas is maintained primarily through tight operational security of the information concerning the attack and an ability to disassociate the perpetrator from the action taken. The members of the ASUs travel separately to their objectives and after an operation will withdraw from the objective separately. Clothes will be changed or dropped off to separate the possible forensic evidence from the guerrilla who will then melt back into the population (British Company Commander 2003). Any weapons or equipment used in an attack will be taken by someone else to dispose of or hide. Reconnaissance of the objective or target will have been performed by a person or persons separate from those who will execute the action to maintain the operational security and disassociation (Fay 2003).

Collaboration with local populace is certainly an IRA strength that has allowed it to maintain urban guerrilla combat operations for many years. The IRA has a sophisticated network of human intelligence collection capabilities perfected through years of operations (Fay 2003). All manner of support comes from different sections of the Catholic populace inside and out of Northern Ireland's borders. Most significant to their urban guerrilla warfare combat operations are reconnaissance and surveillance support. British forces and the RUC are constantly under observation by someone in the IRA's network to keep them informed of their movements (Fay 2003). One of the more obvious civilian IRA supporters encountered by security forces are the "dickers:" teenage boys with cell phones who loiter around security forces' barracks and on the streets, calling in locations and actions of the patrols (British Company Commander 2003). The IRA ensures those who conduct surveillance and reconnaissance are not part of the ASUs and they fall generally into two categories. The first are those who are members of the cause and regularly engage in auxiliary duties, whether they are logistical or intelligence gathering, short of active combat. The other category is simply the sympathetic population, who offer their services or information when asked, but are not truly members of the organization (Fay 2003).

The IRA themselves never wear uniforms except for promotional purposes such as in pictures, on posters, or briefly at funerals for one of its members. This uniform is composed of a black balaclava, a British-type combat jacket, and black pants (Fay 2003). There have been no incidents of using British or RUC uniforms for deception, perhaps because it is considered a dishonorable method of deception (Fay 2003). As recent as 2002, however, a pair of guerrillas gained access to a police barracks using fake or stolen identity cards on a Sunday morning, overpowered a lone guard inside and stole several police files on IRA members (British Company Commander 2003). The issue of conducting operations on non-military targets is really a question of vulnerability. The focus of IRA targets has changed over the years, but the primary target has always been the British military which are symbols of the United Kingdom's occupation of Northern Ireland (Bell 1990). When their focus has changed, such as the bombing campaigns on the mainland, it made for big headlines but also tended to hurt their legitimacy as the military necessity of such targets was more difficult to perceive. The rationale for targeting what appear to most as non-military targets, such as store or hotels, were reasoned away as degrading the British economy (Bell 2000). Criminal activities to finance operations range from extortion and drug-dealing to bank robberies (Marine Corps Intelligence Activity 1999). As the British military and the RUC improved their force protection and intelligence gathering over the years the IRA was forced to focus on more and more vulnerable, yet less military, targets.

The IRA operated in an essentially permissive environment, but with enough British military and RUC presence to keep them outgunned and thus focused on combat operations that did not overly commit their ASUs to direct engagements. Command-detonated bombs, mortars, and sniping were their primary means of prosecuting their attacks as raids and traditional ambushes proved too costly to their limited manpower pool. Small, highly decentralized teams acted with an emphasis on disassociating the guerrilla with the action taken in order to avoid criminal prosecution. Collaboration with the local populace facilitated this disassociation as the auxiliary provided high levels of reconnaissance, transportation, weapons placement and concealment, and exfiltration means for targets. The limited mounted maneuver space and three-dimensional terrain of the urban areas were not issues to the IRA as highly covert, small operations avoided direct combat and large numbers of security forces. Collateral damage to civilian

30

property and persons were involved in their plans and specifically targeted if deemed

profitable, but sometimes hurt their legitimacy when the target strayed too far from the

military and political areas. IRA target selection, both persons and places, is the most

difficult area to reconcile with the Law of War. As the British military and RUC became

more difficult to successfully attack over the years, the IRA moved on to more

vulnerable, less military targets to continue their struggle. The Protocol I requirement to

carry arms openly while deploying for an attack was predominately violated by the IRA,

and would most likely be argued by them to be unreasonable considering the conditions

under which they wage their conflict. These conditions, established as essentially

permissive and termed Urban Operations Under Surgical Conditions by FM 3-06.11,

Combined Arms Operations in Urban Terrain, directly affected the tactics and methods

the IRA used. The strength and capabilities of the military and security forces facing the

IRA and the limited assets available, in terms of manpower and weapons, drove the IRA

to avoid direct confrontation at the tactical level. The next case study will examine a

guerrilla organization under less permissive conditions where large numbers of

government forces were present and security conditions were heightened.

The Mujahideen in Afghanistan

The Soviet Army positioned outposts along all major roads and was especially active in pacifying the northern provinces between Kabul and Termez. Even so, the Kabul regime faced enormous difficulties in ensuring the personal security of its own officials, who were often subject to attacks within the capital itself. The resistance network in Kabul repeatedly carried out shootings, bombings, and assassinations. (Baumann 1993, 136)

Urban combat for the Mujahideen most often consisted of small raids or

ambushes that had more political or psychological effect than military value. Soviets

31

viewed the Mujahideen operations in urban areas as terrorism and sabotage, mostly targeting infrastructure and political objectives. They considered the urban guerrillas who carried out these operations as "diversionary-terrorist" groups, trained across the border in Pakistan to conduct sabotage and terrorist acts (Russian General Staff 2002).

The Mujahideen had great freedom of action in the suburbs and off of the main thoroughfares within the cities, but were often unable to exploit successes due to either their small numbers or lack of organization and planning (Grau and Jalali 1999). Some urban actions occurred in villages and towns that were not occupied by Soviet or Democratic Republic of Afghanistan (DRA) forces. These encounters tended to be under high-intensity conditions, characterized by intense street fighting to maintain control of the terrain (Frunze Academy 1996). In these situations the guerrillas would often use a type of "baited ambush" to lure Soviet forces into the confined streets and passage ways of the villages by establishing initial firing positions on the outskirts and withdrawal into pre-planned defensive positions in and around the adobe walls and buildings (Russian General Staff 2002).

Operational security hindered effectiveness during the rare large-sized raids, such as the raid on the Kabul Metropolitan Bus Transportation Authority which involved 120 Mujahideen fighters, where only the subcommanders knew the plan or final target to preserve security. The bulk of the guerrillas were informed of the plan and their individual duties once they were placed in position (Grau and Jalali 1999). This led to the Mujahideen having detailed plans to get to and from the target but not for actions on the objective.

As with much of the war in Afghanistan, most urban targets had a tactical focus and there seems to have been no effort or plan to tie the targets together with an operational plan. However, at the tactical level different guerrilla bands would conduct combined operations, even between Shia' and Sunni guerrillas. Training the Mujahideen urban guerrillas was very difficult and most training occurred during combat (Grau and Jalali 1999). The urban guerillas that lived outside of the cities or in the suburbs and only came into the city to conduct operations were able to conduct some training in marksmanship or use of the rocket propelled grenade (RPG), but inability to train still remained one of their greatest weaknesses (Grau and Jalali 1999).

The Mujahideen were able to capitalize on the limited mounted maneuver space of the cities through careful reconnaissance. Ambush sites were picked at suburban bazaars known to be frequented by Soviet soldiers upon their departure and return into their base (Grau and Jalali 1999). Often the guerrillas used small teams, consisting of perhaps four men, outfitted with only one RPG. Regardless of whether the plan was to destroy vehicles or not, the Mujahideen always seemed to carry RPGs or other antiarmor weapons with them on urban missions in case they encountered vehicles during their raids or ambushes. No evidence from Soviet or Mujahideen accounts point to any significant use of obstacles by the guerrillas to further degrade vehicular movement in urban areas.

There was no significant use of three-dimensional terrain by the Mujahideen as most of their urban operations remained on the surface and first floors of buildings. During some of the larger urban battles in cities and villages they focused on keeping the fight in the streets to avoid armor, artillery, and air attacks (Russian General Staff 2002).

33

The use of any subsurface areas, such as sewers or subbasements, does not appear in either side's accounts. When possible, some Mujahideen urban guerrillas attacked or infiltrated buildings from the top down. Since many target compounds were surrounded by adobe walls, ladders and ropes were used to scale the perimeter walls then move to the roofs of buildings for entry (Grau and Jalali 1999). When city fighting was expected in the outlying, unoccupied villages and towns the Mujahideen would place crew-served weapons, especially DShKs, on roofs and upper floors (Russian General Staff 2002). The guerrillas displayed no apparent tactics for the clearing or securing of buildings.

The possibility of collateral damage, most often from bomb attacks, seemed to be an acceptable risk to the Mujahideen. Most targets for bombings or RPG attacks on buildings were Soviet, DRA, or communist party officials. As Mr. Grau points out in his commentary of an urban bombing attack in *The Other Side of the Mountain*, the only real difference between bombing attacks and aerial bombardments is the size of the bomb and the means of delivery. Although most noncombatant casualties that did occur happened as a result of the bombings, aimed at communist party officials and their office workers, other incidents did happen. During one failed raid on a telephone exchange center the Mujahideen attacked the compound's security force with small arms during their chaotic withdrawal and learned later that they had killed some of the sentries' relatives that were staying with them (Grau and Jalali 1999).

Although snipers were most likely used by urban Mujahideen guerrillas to some degree, there is almost no mention of them in either Mujahideen or Soviet accounts. This leads to a conclusion that, if used, they were of very small effect on operations for either side. This could be due to a lack of sufficient marksmanship training necessary to develop a proficient sniper.

Congruent with all successful guerrilla operations, the element of surprise was the decisive factor in the Mujahideen's ability to conduct successful combat operations in urban environments. This was primarily through the use of civilian contacts and auxiliary to prepare the area for operations, either through reconnaissance or actually aiding in the execution of the action (Grau and Jalali 1999). The Mujahideen were very adept in planning for their infiltration into and exfiltration away from their objectives. Ambush and raid sites were often selected in conjunction with the routes to and from Mujahideen bases and safe houses to ensure concealed movement. Infiltrations were most often made through the suburbs with their knowledge of the city's friendly, enemy, and neutral areas to guide their planning (Grau and Jalali 1999). Most movements were made on foot even on their approaches into the cities from rural areas. Once inside the suburbs they were able to move quickly through the streets because of their knowledge of the areas and the enemy rarely ventured into these areas which were considered unsecure. When necessary, the Mujahideen were able to quickly gather large numbers of guerrillas (up to 130) for missions that required it, sometimes from different guerrilla bands (Grau and Jalali 1999). The guerrillas rarely stayed on target very long after the attack for fear of quick reaction forces. Their rapid withdrawal capability came from their route security and prior reconnaissance of the objective area. The guerrillas used outlying villages as mission support sites to consolidate, gather and prepare equipment, and finalize plans before moving to the target area.

Security for the Mujahideen urban combat operations played a predominant role in their planning. Heavy security was used on the routes into and out of the objective areas, sometimes consisting of as much as 70-80 percent of the total force available. However, many cities had curfews at various times during the conflict which could make large numbers of security personnel stand out during the night (Grau and Jalali 1999). Urban operations left little time for prisoner of war searches, gathering intelligence, equipment retrieval, or damage assessments because the proximity of security forces dictated rapid withdrawal of forces to preserve their strength. During withdrawals the Mujahideen would separate into small groups and move by different routes to assembly areas (Russian General Staff 2002). Detailed reconnaissance, often for several days, gave the Mujahideen knowledge of the enemy's movement and security arrangements and contributed to their ability to conduct many missions in the heart of Soviet or DRA garrisoned areas (Grau and Jalali 1999). As opposed to their rural guerrilla counterparts, the urban guerrillas were able to spend more time in reconnaissance and surveillance of their targets to determine patterns and vulnerabilities (Russian General Staff 2002). Their ability to move about in the local urban populace gave them this advantage whereas the rural guerrilla was forced to remain in hiding while not conducting operations. Isolation of the objective areas was almost always taken in consideration. Many of the security forces that took up the bulk of the manpower on operations were kept as security and blocking forces on the objective. Many of the garrisoned targets had security posts on their exterior or along the route to them (Grau and Jalali 1999). The Mujahideen would post security details at each of these posts to ensure they were not revealed on their way into the target or ambushed on their way out. Small teams of security were placed along the routes of infiltration and exfiltration. Larger security teams were placed as blocking positions in the vicinity of the target against any reaction forces.

Collaboration with the local populace gave the urban Mujahideen guerrillas the access they needed to penetrate high value Soviet and DRA targets (Grau and Jalali 1999). The use of contacts inside government buildings or enemy military garrisons often meant that contact had to leave and join the Mujahideen as their assistance was often direct (bomb emplacement, letting guerrillas in while on sentry duty for the DRA, etc.). The Mujahideen used civilians who worked in target buildings to emplace and arm bombs. Contacts within military (Soviet or DRA) and government (communist party) buildings were used to provide essential information on the inside of target buildings such as the number of security forces or the schedule of the work force. Local civilians were occasionally used as guides but most often the guerrillas knew the cities well enough that guides were not needed. Local contacts, essentially auxiliary members, often provided security for small missions such as a five-man assault team (Grau and Jalali 1999). Local auxiliary would also provide safe houses for movement through the cities.

The urban Mujahideen wore no uniforms or distinctive insignia and intentionally blurred the line between combatant and non-combatant to deceive the Soviets and Afghan government forces. Elderly citizens were used to carry messages and explosives and civilian workers, sometimes even females, planted bombs in government offices (Grau and Jalali 1999). The use of enemy uniforms for deception was used in some circumstances. During one example a guerrilla dressed as a DRA officer in order to kidnap a Soviet advisor. One group even dressed as civilian farmers and sold fruit and vegetables from a cart to Soviet advisors at a bus stop for several days (Grau and Jalali

37

1999). The cart was outfitted with a false bottom and loaded with explosives and timed fuses that detonated when a crowd of Soviets was around it. Nonmilitary targets were also attacked when considered necessary to display the Mujahideen's control over the urban situation or when it would have some impact on Soviet or DRA command and control in the cities. Examples such as the attacks on a bus terminal and the telephone exchange center were conducted to disrupt daily life in the city and show that the Soviets and DRA were not able to stop them (Grau and Jalali 1999).

The urban Mujahideen operated in a semipermissive environment in the cities as most of the heavy combat during the conflict was in the rural areas of Afghanistan. Encounters between Mujahideen and Soviet or DRA forces in small villages and towns not normally occupied by government security forces tended to be high-intensity, characterized by street fighting and conventional offensive and defensive tactics to gain or maintain control of the urban terrain. The guerrilla operations conducted in the larger Soviet and Afghan government controlled cities like Kabul or Kandahar displayed the tactics and methods of the Mujahideen urban guerrilla. These tactics focused on small raids, ambushes, and bombings with extensive reconnaissance and a heavy emphasis on security. In fact, security for combat operations in the cities used the majority of guerrilla forces available to the Mujahideen. The guerrilla often used 60-70 percent of available forces to secure routes into and out of the objective area as the possibility of being ambushed or surprised during operations in the urban areas was greatly increased. Although the security plans were well thought out, many Mujahideen urban operations were characterized by poor actions on the objective, either from a lack of planning or tactical proficiency. The limited mounted maneuver space and three-dimensional terrain of the cities was utilized by the guerrillas, but not to a large degree. Through careful reconnaissance of ambush sites the guerrillas ensured that Soviet vehicles would have a difficult time maneuvering once attacked and any quick reaction forces would be delayed in responding. Collateral damage to civilian property and persons was avoided, unless associated with the communist government, which was considered as much an enemy as the Soviets. The urban Mujahideen's collaboration with the local populace and also with Afghans within the government or DRA provided much of their access to Soviet and government installations and offered essential information concerning security forces, guard schedules, and the like. The urban guerrillas, as a matter of survival, did not openly carry arms while deploying for attacks, especially bombings. Their targets were predominantly military, however non-military targets were attacked to display Mujahideen control of the urban centers or if it would adversely impact on Soviet or DRA command and control. The semipermissive conditions the urban Mujahideen operated under, essentially the Urban Operations Under Precision Conditions as outlined by FM 3-06.11, *Combined Arms Operations in Urban Terrain*, allowed the Mujahideen more access to military targets within the cities. The presence of large numbers of security forces, both Soviet and DRA, also drove the guerrillas to at times operate in larger elements than the IRA. The final case study will examine a guerrilla organization under non-permissive urban conditions and under high-intensity combat.

The Chechen Rebels in Grozny

Where the Russians fought to control and hold the territory, the rebels fought to make controlling and holding the territory as unpleasant as possible--a very different mission, and one far more difficult both to grasp and to counter. (Oliker 2001, 73)

The battles for Grozny, especially in 1994-95, were high-intensity urban combat the likes of which the Russians had not seen since their World War II battles against the Germans. The Russians had not envisioned the level of conflict to be as violent as it became and had put together ad hoc units to move into Grozny to disarm the Chechen rebels (Kulikov 2001). Although the Russian experience in Chechnya would eventually spread out to include the rural areas, it began under high-intensity urban combat in Grozny.

The Chechens were extremely effective during small unit battles with the Russian forces by utilizing methods with which the Russians were either unfamiliar or unable to counter. Using the tactic of "hugging" the rebels would stay close to the Russian units as they moved to avoid indirect fire and keep at close range (Thomas 1999). The guerrilla mortar crews would also move constantly, firing three to four rounds then displacing to avoid counter-battery fire (Oliker 2001). Both of these techniques significantly reduced Russian fire support as an effective tool against the guerrillas when in direct contact. Although the rebels had some night vision equipment, either left behind by the army earlier in the 1990s or stolen from Russian units, it was not commonplace among the guerrillas. Yet the Chechens were able to operate effectively at night while the Russians preferred not to (Oliker 2001). Operations were predominately conducted by small units of three to eight personnel, growing up to seventy-five man groups for planned large-scale ambushes. Some exceptions existed, such as Shamil Basayev's "national guard," composed of some 500 battle-hardened veterans of the Abkhazian-Georgian conflict, who sometimes operated in groups as large as 200 (Thomas 1999). Many Chechen rebels were veterans of the Soviet Army and understood the Russian tactics, capabilities, and weaknesses. Interestingly, the Chechens did not use tracers as they felt it revealed their locations. The Russians eventually adapted this also as Chechen snipers were able to target them in the day and night by their tracer fire (Marine Corps Intelligence Activity 1999).

Chechen command and control was very loose and although the Presidential Palace was fortified and heavily defended the rebels did not concentrate forces in the center of the city (Oliker 2001). The defensive preparation of Grozny had begun three to four months prior to Russian operations commencing and the defense of Grozny was composed generally of three concentric zones. The inner zone consisted of the fortified presidential palace and the immediate one to two kilometers around it. A middle zone extending up to an additional five kilometers focused on strongpoints covering key terrain and avenues of approach to the center of the city. The outer zone consisted of the perimeter and outskirts of the city for reconnaissance, surveillance, and harassment of Russian forces (Oliker 2001). The loose command and control structure emphasized small, mobile groups able to quickly react to Russian operations.

The Chechens were able to capitalize on the limited mounted maneuver space to defeat the Russian advantage in armored vehicles. Due to their familiarity with the equipment, the rebels targeted the fuel cells and engines of the Russian armored vehicles. They focused their fire on the top, sides, and rear to avoid the reactive armor (Oliker 2001). The rebels used multiple RPG teams against Russian vehicles to overcome the problems of backblast signature and reloading time while simultaneously disorienting the Russians as to the direction of the attack (Oliker 2001). Small anti-tank "hunter-killer" teams, armed with several RPGs, roamed the city listening for engine noise. They would then converge on the vehicles and volley fire from multiple directions, including above (Marine Corps Intelligence Activity 1999). Lack of Russian infantry support, especially early on in the battle, contributed to this success. The Chechens had some tanks and artillery pieces most of which were used at various strongpoints to counter Russian armored attacks. RPGs were the primary anti-armor weapon and seemingly every unit, from a three-man team to the 75-man planned ambush units, carried them in large amounts. At the various strongpoints and especially around the presidential palace obstacles such as destroyed vehicles and debris were used, primarily to funnel the Russians into engagement areas. These areas were covered by the tanks and direct-fire artillery (Kulikov 2001). In the 2000 battle a lot of time was spent digging antitank ditches (Thomas 2000). Mobile detachments in civilian vehicles or jeeps transported supplies, ammunition, weapons, and troops throughout the city.

The Chechens' masterful use of three-dimensional terrain was a constant problem for Russian progress in the city. The rebels boarded up or blocked first floor entrances to buildings to deny their use by the Russians, allowing them little or no cover once an engagement began on the street (Speyer 2001). Passages through the buildings were made for maneuver and withdrawal routes (Oliker 2001). Below the surface the rebels constructed and used a network of underground passages, subbasements, and bunkers. Basement window positions would be used to attack armor since their guns tubes could not depress enough to engage the attackers. These positions would be reinforced into bunkers and car jacks were used to raise and lower concrete slabs and other reinforced roofing material, allowing the rebels to fire on passing vehicles and troops and then avoid the retaliatory indirect fire by lowering the slabs (Oliker 2001). It is unclear whether the

42

city's sewer system was used by the rebels. Russian reports say it was, but the Chechens deny its use (Oliker 2001). Roofs and top floors were generally left empty for fear of air attacks and artillery. The rebels then attacked from the middle floors and used preplanned withdrawal routes (Speyer 2001). Buildings were used for strongpoints when defending key terrain. In other areas the Chechens occupied buildings as needed to escape concentrated Russian fires or to draw them into engagement areas and kill zones. Except for perhaps the Presidential Palace, defended buildings were not seen as crucial to the Chechen defense. Rather, making the Russians suffer a disparity of casualties and damage for a small piece of terrain was the objective.

Collateral damage to non-military targets and personnel did not appear to overly concern the Chechen rebels. They would deploy near a school or hospital, engage the Russian forces, and then quickly move away. The Russians would shell the area from which they received fire, inevitably destroying the nonmilitary targets (Marine Corps Intelligence Activity 1999). The Chechens would then later use this as propaganda against the Russians. It is unclear whether these civilian targets were occupied by non-combatants or not when used by the Chechens in this fashion. Most of the collateral damage to the city was done by the Russians through artillery fire and airstrikes, especially in the 2000 battle, when the city was essentially leveled in an effort to avoid the brutal street fighting that was encountered in 1994.

Snipers were a key and very effective element of the urban guerrilla operations conducted by the Chechens. They often targeted radiomen and officers (Oliker 2001). The basic fighting unit of three to eight personnel almost always included a sniper, meaning almost every engagement the Russians had included having to deal with a sniper

(Oliker 2001). They were positioned and fired from deep within rooms to avoid detection, and were used as scouts as much as for sniping. One tactic would be to shoot Russian soldiers in the leg then engage those who attempted to help, further complicating Russian casualty evacuation and often forcing it to be conducted only at night (Oliker 2001). The psychological effect of the snipers was just as great, or greater, than their physical contribution (Speyer 2001). They were highly feared by the Russian soldiers and operated in both the day and night (Oliker 2001). Snipers were often used to draw Russian forces into baited ambushes (Speyer 2001). They were also used to control the approaches to specific intersections from roofs or upper floors (Thomas 2000).

Surprise was achieved primarily by the Chechens operating in small, mobile groups that could react to Russian movements and operations as they chose. Deception planning became a key to maintaining surprise by monitoring Russian movements and drawing them into the center of the city by offering little or weak resistance (Speyer 2001). Street signs were taken down or repositioned to confuse Russian movements (Thomas 1999). The rebels were able to move into and out of Grozny quite freely in 1995 since the Russians did not seal off the city until late into the battle. This ability was severely lessened in 2000 as the Russians had learned their lesson and sealed off the city in the beginning. The Chechens maintained their speed of movement and mobility by not having many strong points and consistently moving in small groups, harassing the Russians when opportunities arose (Thomas 1999). Civilian vehicles with mounted 23 millimeter cannons or 12.7 millimeter heavy machineguns were used to quickly position air defense assets around the city. The guerrillas demonstrated the ability to rapidly concentrate their forces when needed to counter Russian operations even with their loose

44

command and control. Even though their small teams of three to eight personnel often operated independently, the rebels seemed to be able to mass when necessary or when in anticipation of a particular Russian operation, to include maintaining interconnected fire positions (Marine Corps Intelligence Activity 1999). The Chechen guerrillas communicated with civilian off-the-shelf radios using their native language, for which the Russians had few translators, which added to this capability to concentrate forces quickly. The rebels always had preplanned escape routes from firing positions. Some mortars were mounted in civilian trucks to improve their tactical mobility and defend against counterbattery fire (Marine Corps Intelligence Activity 1999). Tunnels between buildings and hidden subbasements also allowed the rebels to move quickly between positions or wait and hide as the Russians moved through, surfacing later behind the Russians in areas considered cleared.

Security for the Chechens was their mobility. The confusion of urban combat allowed them to drift into and out of contact with the Russians almost at will. Unlike urban combat in less intense conditions where a guerrilla's movements must be more covert to avoid detection by the populace as well as the enemy, most of the population left in Grozny was ethnic Chechens and not a threat to the rebels. When necessary they would blend in with civilians having been moments before, engaged in a firefight with Russian troops. Their ability to maintain constant reconnaissance and surveillance throughout the suburbs gave them early warning of most of the Russian movements (Speyer 2001). The Chechens would also isolate critical points when conducting large ambushes. They would use two-thirds of the force for security with one twenty-five man element conducting the ambush and two twenty-five man elements sealing off the objective and engaging follow-on forces (Oliker 2001).

Since most of the civilians in Grozny were ethnic Chechens and sympathetic to the rebels' cause, their collaboration with the local populace was complete from the beginning. The rebels even moved their operations to successive cities after Grozny to maintain the urban advantage and keep the population on their side because the Russians destroyed property and killed noncombatants in their efforts to secure urban areas. Initially, when the Russians were trying to minimize civilian casualties, the rebels were able to use the population actively by stopping Russian convoys, puncturing tires, and generally interfering with their operations, but the Russians eventually caught on and increased their security (Marine Corps Intelligence Activity 1999). The rebels routinely used the population for information gathering and young women proved especially useful since they could easily move throughout the city and make contact with the Russians (Speyer 2001).

The Chechen use of uniforms was haphazard and varied between the different bands that made up the rebels. Some rebels had Russian uniforms from their time in the Soviet or Russian military (Thomas 2000a), and were used more out of necessity than intent to deceive. Generally, the rebels rarely wore uniforms and were difficult to distinguish (Speyer 2001). Reports from the 2000 battle said that rebels dressed as Russian soldiers for night raids on Russian positions, but there is little corroborating evidence of this. Other accounts had Russian-dressed rebels committing atrocities against civilians to discredit the Russians (Oliker 2001). Chechens sometimes disguised themselves as Red Cross workers, donning the armbands and moving freely among the

46

Russian soldiers (Thomas 1999). The rebels would also offer themselves as civilian guides and lead the Russians into ambushes (Oliker 2001). The use of nonmilitary targets by the rebels could be seen while discussing collateral damage and their intentional use of protected property such as hospitals to draw Russian fire, thus claiming Russian atrocities. The Chechens also targeted Russian aerial and ground medical evacuation vehicles. Some reports say rebels took Chechen hostages to coerce their family members to serve as artillery spotters in the Russian rear (Thomas 1999).

The Chechens operated under nonpermissive, high-intensity combat conditions where the Russian forces' objective was to seize and control Grozny. Predominately operating in small teams, the guerrillas controlled the tempo of the engagements by their tactic of hugging the Russian forces: staying at close range to maintain pressure on the Russian units and simultaneously avoiding airpower and indirect fire. Direct fire ambushes were the most often used method of attack. The ambushes were often executed by the small, mobile teams armed with multiple RPGs who roved the city looking for targets of opportunity. Large, planned ambushes were also conducted and focused on sealing off the kill zone with blocking forces and attacking the Russians with heavy RPG and machine gun fire. The limited mounted maneuver space and three-dimensional terrain was highly capitalized on by the Chechens. As Russian vehicles were baited into areas of reduced maneuverability they were ambushed from basement windows, the street-level, and multi-story building positions that targeted vulnerable areas on the Russian vehicles. Collateral damage did overly concern the Chechens but they understood the ramifications it would have on Russian operations and capitalized on this by deploying their troops or equipment near schools and hospitals. Sniper operations

47

played a dominant role in the Chechen defense of Grozny and were greatly feared by the Russians. Sniping was so important to the guerrillas that the basic unit of the Chechens, the three to eight man team, always had at least one sniper on it. The guerrillas' collaboration with the local populace increased their combat effectiveness, but was less of a crucial factor than in the earlier case studies. The nature of the high-intensity combat of the battles of Grozny meant a smaller role for covert use of civilians because, although useful, it was not required to get close or gain access to the Russian targets. The Chechens blurred the line of clear distinction by sometimes donning Russian uniforms or Red Cross armbands. The high-intensity combat conditions meant that they predominately carried their arms openly during military engagements although at times they did deceive the Russians by acting as civilian guides and leading them into ambushes. FM 3-06.11, *Combined Arms Operations in Urban Terrain*, would qualify the conditions in Grozny as Urban Operations Under High-Intensity Conditions. The Chechens therefore operated at a less covert and clandestine role than the previous case studies. Direct confrontation and engagement of Russian forces was necessary to defend Grozny, and the urban guerrilla tactics offset the imbalance the Chechens faced in manpower and conventional weapons and equipment.

Current Special Forces Doctrine

Analyzing current Special Forces TTP for conducting urban guerrilla warfare combat operations is not difficult because there is none. The question then, in reference to the primary question to be answered in the final chapter, is if it is needed. There is plentiful TTP concerning guerrilla combat operations which are focused on rural environments. The principles and characteristics for particular combat operations do not change. For instance, an ambush, a surprise attack on a moving or temporarily halted enemy, should possess assault, support, and security elements of some fashion. Current Special Forces TTP for ambushes cover several techniques and methods to conduct an ambush as well as the governing principles and characteristics for this and other combat operations involving guerrillas.

One anticipated outcome from the analyzed case studies which proved to be true was that many of the tactics and techniques utilized by the studied guerrillas were really examples of utilizing good tactical sense, and not some special urban method of guerrilla warfare. As one Russian officer, a veteran of the battles for Grozny, stated in a presentation to US officers, the Chechens had used "sound tactical principles" (Presentation 2002). For instance, using a baited ambush to lure enemy forces into pursuing guerrillas into an established kill zone was used in one form or another by all three guerrilla organizations. This was a technique I used as an opposing force platoon leader at the Joint Readiness Training Center against units rotating in for training and is easily modified for use in an urban environment. This outcome reinforces that TTPs are merely methods that facilitate the principles of combat operations and leverage the conditions under which you must apply those principles.

An unanticipated outcome was that, except for the IRA case study, bomb attacks played a lesser role than is generally thought when one envisions an urban guerrilla struggle. The IRA has used the bomb as a primary means of attack quite extensively, but even their use of mortars and snipers was greater than anticipated. The Mujahideen utilized bombing as a viable weapon in their urban conflict but a large percentage of their combat operations were both small and large raids and ambushes. The Chechens seemed

49

to utilize very little bombing and predominately engaged in direct combat through ambushes and sniping. This demonstrates that bombing, although effective, is not the only viable combat operation option available to the urban guerrilla. Bombing, although it protects the guerrilla who conducts it by disassociation, can be inaccurate and turn an insurgency into a terrorist act in world opinion through intentional or unintended collateral damage.

Following the criteria established in chapter 3 which was taken from US doctrinal characteristics of urban environments, guerrilla warfare, and relevant legal aspects of war, each case study was analyzed for how the guerrillas conducted their combat operations in urban environments. Having now analyzed how the guerrillas conducted their urban operations and what their TTPs were, the final question to be answered is whether urban guerrilla warfare TTP should be included in Special Forces doctrine.

CHAPTER 5

CONCLUSIONS AND RECOMMENDATIONS

The purpose of this chapter is to answer the primary question, Does Special

Forces doctrine for guerrilla warfare combat operations tactics, techniques, and

procedures need modifications or additions for application in urban environments?

Previous chapters answered secondary questions by establishing the three researched case

studies as examples of guerrilla warfare with significant urban combat activities. The

TTP for rural and urban guerrilla warfare combat operations in current Special Forces

doctrine was also established in these chapters. Most importantly, the tertiary questions

were answered by examining the tactics and methods utilized by each case study in

conducting their guerrilla combat operations in urban environments. The analysis of this

information indicates that Special Forces doctrine does need guerrilla warfare combat

operations TTP for urban environments. To demonstrate this we need to examine the

results of research interpretations.

Research Interpretation Conclusions

The environmental aspects of the urban areas forced each of the researched

guerrilla organizations to develop specific TTP to overcome the disadvantages they faced

in the cities. The IRA had a small manpower pool in the cities to attack the British

military and RUC forces, which always had nearby units for backup, and had to contend

with the police forensics that could connect them to attacks after the fact. In order to

avoid direct engagement with security forces and escape criminal prosecution if captured,

they developed and utilized tactics that disassociated the guerrilla from the act of violence. The Mujahideen also had to overcome the large numbers of Russian and DRA military forces in the urban centers who were often enclosed in secure compounds. They countered the threat of enemy quick reaction and security forces in the cities with extensive security of their own, often utilizing the majority of forces available, and close collaboration with the local population to gain access to enemy compounds. As the Chechen rebels prepared to defend Grozny they correctly identified the Russians' tremendous advantage in firepower and their ability to destroy or seize defensive positions as their strength. To overcome the imbalance in firepower, the Chechens operated in small, mobile teams that struck the Russians quickly and then just as quickly dissipated into the depths of the city. During firefights they stayed close to the Russian units to avoid indirect fire and close air support.

The urban environment also offered the guerrilla certain advantages the rural areas could not. One of the most obvious advantages is that of drawing attention to the guerrillas' cause, whatever it may be. As FM 3-05.201, *Special Forces Unconventional Warfare Operations* (Initial Draft), states in the appendix dedicated to unconventional warfare in urban environments, the political institutions and communication media are located in its urban centers, with their controls centered in this seat of power. When a guerrilla organization conducts operations in the cities it ensures that the mass of the population, and the outside world, are aware of its existence and capabilities. This is an operational or strategic advantage to guerrilla warfare in urban areas but can assist the tactical operations by increased recruiting, support from outside organizations or nations, and increased internal or external pressure on the enemy to resolve the conflict on favorable terms to the guerrillas.

There were also tactical advantages that the urban environment offered the guerrillas. Operating in the cities afforded the guerrillas greater contact with large numbers of the endorsing population and thus all the associated support they could offer. Critical to this support was the urban reconnaissance of the auxiliary and especially the access it provided to enemy installations and command organizations. The three-dimensional terrain also gave the guerrilla tactical advantages. Sometimes this was manifested in methods of concealment or withdrawal from objectives that the built-up areas provided. Often the three-dimensional terrain allowed the guerrillas to get very close to their enemy during combat operations and eliminate the advantage in firepower and range the conventional forces usually enjoyed. Another advantage for the guerrillas was that the urban combat was predominately conducted by small units as the terrain restricted the movement, visibility, and communications of their enemies. This aspect significantly affected the force ratios facing each of the guerrilla organizations in the case studies, and allowed them to even the odds to a great degree.

Each of the guerrilla organizations in the researched case studies also faced particular legal issues, whether they knew or cared about them or not, due to the urban terrain in which they were fighting. Combat of any kind, guerrilla or otherwise, in the cities will bring the combatants within close proximity of the civilian population. The Law of War concept of protected persons and property becomes a constant issue in urban areas, far more frequently than the occasional farmer and church encountered in the countryside. The concept of distinction between combatant and noncombatant makes it very difficult for the guerrilla to operate in the cities and still remain in accordance with the Law of War. He must be able to blend in with the populace, or at a minimum remain concealed, when not conducting operations. Tactically, guerrilla combatants must abide by the Law of War in order to be afforded Geneva Convention rights if they are captured and become prisoners of war, thereby keeping them immune from their war-like acts. From a strategic viewpoint, the ability of a guerrilla organization to follow the Law of War and abide by the Geneva Conventions will give them greater legitimacy regionally and globally, and would certainly be a serious issue in determining US support to an insurgency. The relevance of these legal issues is that while they will always be of concern during guerrilla warfare operations, they will be especially important during urban guerrilla warfare because of the density of the civilian population and the increased attention that conflict in urban centers brings.

An aspect that could not be addressed by these case studies is how US Special Forces soldiers would operate with their indigenous or surrogate forces in the conduct of urban guerrilla warfare. One issue that has always plagued the concept of urban guerrilla warfare involving US Special Forces is how an individual with obvious American or western features would be able to remain hidden or inconspicuous in a city filled with people of a significantly different ethnicity. The Jedburgh teams of the Office of Strategic Services, Special Forces predecessors in World War II, did not have too much trouble with this in Western Europe because they were ethnically similar. Today's Special Forces, operating in the contemporary environment, are working all over the world and would certainly stand out in a city like downtown Jakarta. Solutions to this dilemma would be dependent on the region and conditions that were encountered. The case studies did not have external military support or assistance similar to that which US Special Forces would bring to a guerrilla organization. However, what each case study did demonstrate is that an urban guerrilla warfare campaign can be waged by keeping the auxiliary within the confines of the city to conduct support and reconnaissance and having the overt military arm of the insurgency, the guerrillas, come in only to conduct combat operations.

Comparison of the TTP of current Special Forces doctrine for guerrilla warfare combat operations and the researched TTP of the case studies points to the obvious conclusion that the current doctrine does not address the urban environment. The current TTP for guerrilla warfare combat operations is tactically sound and is based on established principles of light infantry combat operations. It is, however, meant to be employed in rural terrain. What the current TTP does not offer are methods and techniques of applying those established principles in the urban environment by countering the disadvantages and leveraging the advantages that the city offers to the guerrilla. These conclusions demonstrate that in each of the case studies the guerrillas had to develop and utilize TTP for combat operations that could be used in the urban areas because that environment possessed aspects, both good and bad, that their rural methods could not address.

Significance of Conclusions

The case studies demonstrate a phenomenon that has been written about in Special Forces doctrine for decades. Chapter 2 addressed the past Special Forces doctrinal manuals that since the 1960s have described urban guerrilla warfare as a viable method as opposed to the traditional rural insurgency. The current doctrinal manuals for both Army and Special Forces operations stress the effect global urbanization will have on future operations. So whereas it is firmly established in Special Forces doctrine that

55

urban guerrilla warfare is a contemporary and viable reality, there is no guidance on how to conduct it at the tactical level.

Differing rural environments, such as jungle, arctic, or desert terrain require adjustments usually related to cover, concealment and observation. The urban environment, however, possesses aspects not found in varying rural areas such as three-dimensional terrain and proximity of civilians. The conventional army devotes two field manuals and one training circular specifically focused on training for and conducting operations in urban environments. Many of the principles of the conventional combat operations are generally the same, but the environment itself poses particular problems that need to be addressed with new, different, or adjusted TTP. Guerrilla warfare operations are no different. The tactical principles are the same, but specific TTP for the urban environment must be used for the guerrilla to survive and win in this complex environment.

The urban environment has increasingly become a focus of the US Army, and rightly so. Every military operation the US undertook in the 1990s involved operating in built-up areas to some level, from peacekeeping duties of the Balkans to high-intensity street fighting in Somalia. There are also many examples in the twentieth century of urban insurgencies, all with varying levels of intensity regarding the guerrilla warfare combat operations that were conducted. Unconventional warfare is the primary mission of US Special Forces. While conducting this mission in the contemporary environment, Special Forces soldiers most likely will have to employ many or all of the aspects of unconventional warfare in the urban environment. When conducting guerrilla warfare, the overt military aspect of unconventional warfare, in urban areas the Special Forces soldier must be able to address the characteristics of urban terrain while following the principles of guerrilla warfare and utilizing methods that do not violate the Law of War. Establishing urban guerrilla warfare combat operations TTP in doctrine will allow him to do this.

<u>Recommendations for Further Study</u>

Further research into other historical examples of urban guerrilla warfare would reinforce and compliment those done in this thesis. There are many cases such as the Tupamaros in Uruguay, the Monteneros in Argentina, and the National Liberation Front in Algeria that would offer even more aspects of urban guerrilla tactics. The difficulty is determining how the guerrillas conducted their urban combat operations - - their literal techniques and methods. Few guerrillas conduct written after action reports. Consequently, although we often know from history what they did, it is more difficult to determine how they did it.

Urban guerrilla warfare TTPs should be included in the appendix dedicated to unconventional warfare in FM 3-05.201, *Special Forces Unconventional Warfare Operations*. Just as the TTPs for rural combat operations, the urban TTPs should describe the principles and characteristics that are common in their employment, to include the procedures, with accompanying diagrams, for various urban ambush, raid, sniper, and bombing techniques. If necessary, this information may need to have a restricted distribution of some level but all of the information used in this thesis was gained from open source documents or unclassified interviews. Legal issues pertaining to urban guerrilla warfare, such as the use of civilian clothes and visible arms, should be included in the legal considerations appendix of FM 3-05.201.

REFERENCE LIST

Baumann, Robert F. 1993. *Leavenworth Papers 20: Russian-Soviet Unconventional Wars in the Caucasus, Central Asia, and Afghanistan.* Washington, DC: US Government Printing Office.

Baldy, Tom F. 1987. *Battle for Ulster: A Study of Internal Security.* Washington, DC: National Defense University Press.

Bell, J. Bowyer. 1990. *IRA Tactics and Targets.* Dublin, Ireland: Poolbeg Press Ltd.

Bell, J. Bowyer. 2000. *The IRA 1968-2000: Analysis of a Secret Army.* Portland, OR: Frank Cass Publishers.

Black, Robert J. 1972. A Change in Tactics? The Urban Insurgent. *Air University Review* 23, no. 2 (January-February 1972): 50-58.

British Company Commander, Major. 2003. Interview by author. Written recording. Name withheld upon request. Fort Leavenworth, Kansas.

Clutterbuck, Richard L. 1990. *Terrorism and Guerrilla Warfare: Forecasts and Remedies.* New York, NY: Routledge.

Department of the Army. 1951a. FM 31-20, *Operations Against Guerilla Forces.* Washington, DC: US Government Printing Office.

_____. 1951b. FM 31-21, *Organization and Conduct of Guerrilla Warfare.* Washington, DC: US Government Printing Office.

_____. 1955a. FM 31-20, *US Army Special Forces Group (Airborne) (U).* Washington, DC: US Government Printing Office.

_____. 1955b. FM 31-21, *Guerilla Warfare.* Washington, DC: US Government Printing Office.

_____. 1958a. FM 21-77, *Evasion and Escape.* Washington, DC: US Government Printing Office.

_____. 1958b. FM 31-21, *Guerrilla Warfare and Special Forces Operations.* Washington, DC: US Government Printing Office.

_____. 1961. FM 31-21, *Guerrilla Warfare and Special Forces Operations.* Washington, DC: US Government Printing Office.

_____. 1965. FM 31-20, *Special Forces Operational Techniques*. Washington, DC: US Government Printing Office.

_____. 1969. FM 31-21, *Special Forces Operations - US Army Doctrine*. Washington, DC: US Government Printing Office.

_____. 1971. FM 31-20, *Special Forces Operational Techniques*. Washington, DC: US Government Printing Office.

_____. 1978. ST 31-201, *Special Forces Operations*. Washington, DC: US Government Printing Office.

_____. 1988. TC 31-29, *Special Forces Operational Techniques*. Washington, DC: US Government Printing Office.

_____. 1990. FM 31-20, *Doctrine for Special Forces Operations - US Army Doctrine*. Washington, DC: US Government Printing Office.

_____. 1993. FM 31-20-5, *Special Reconnaissance Tactics, Techniques, and Procedures for Special Forces*. Washington, DC: US Government Printing Office.

_____. 1994. FM 31-20-3, *Foreign Internal Defense Tactics, Techniques, and Procedures for Special Forces*. Washington, DC: US Government Printing Office.

_____. 1999. FM 100-25, *Doctrine for Army Special Operations Forces*. Washington, DC: US Government Printing Office.

_____. 2001a. FM 3.05-20, *Special Forces Operations*. Washington, DC: US Government Printing Office.

_____. 2001b. FM 3.05-201, *Special Forces Unconventional Warfare Operations (Initial Draft)*. Washington, DC: US Government Printing Office.

_____. 2001c. FM 3-06.1, *Aviation Urban Operations*. Washington, DC: US Government Printing Office.

_____. 2002a. FM 3-06.11, *Combined Arms Operations in Urban Terrain*. Washington, DC: US Government Printing Office.

_____. 2002b. *Operational Law Handbook*. Washington, DC: US Government Printing Office.

_____. 2002c. TC 90-1, *Training for Urban Operations*. Washington, DC: US Government Printing Office.

Department of Defense. 2001. Joint Publication 1-02, *Department of Defense Dictionary of Military and Associated Terms*. Washington, DC: US Government Printing Office.

Derradji, Abder-Rahmane. 1997. *The Algerian Guerrilla Campaign: Strategy and Tactics*. Lewiston, NY: The Edwin Mellen Press.

Ellis, John. 1976. *A Short History of Guerrilla Warfare*. New York, NY: St. Martin's Press.

Fay, Angus, Lt Col, British Army. 2003. Interview by author. Written recording. Fort Leavenworth, Kansas.

Finch, Raymond C., III. 1998. *Why the Russian Military Failed in Chechnya*. Foreign Military Studies Office Special Study no. 98-16. Fort Leavenworth, KS: Center For Army Lessons Learned.

Frunze Academy. 1996. *The Bear Went Over the Mountain: Soviet Combat Tactics in Afghanistan*. Translated and edited by Lester W. Grau. Washington, DC: National Defense University Press.

General Headquarters. 1985. *Handbook for Volunteers of the Irish Republican Army: Notes on Guerrilla Warfare*. Boulder, CO: Paladin Press.

Grau, Lester W. 1997. Russian Manufactured Armored Vehicle Vulnerability in Urban Combat: The Chechnya Experience. *Red Thrust Star*. January 1997. Available from http://fmso.leavenworth.army.mil/RED-STAR/issues/JAN97/ JAN97.HTML.

Grau, Lester W. and William A. Jorgenson, D.O. 1998. Handling the Wounded in a Counter-Guerrilla War: the Soviet/Russian Experience in Afghanistan and Chechnya. *US Army Medical Department Journal*. January-February 1998. Available from http://fmso.leavenworth.army.mil/fmsopubs/issues/handlwnd/ handlwnd.htm.

Grau, Lester W. 1998. The RPG-7 On the Battlefields of Today and Tomorrow. *Infantry*. Vol. 88, no. 2, May-August 1998: 6-8.

Grau, Lester W. and Ali Ahmed Jalali. 1999. *The Other Side of the Mountain: Mujahideen Tactics in the Soviet-Afghan War*. Quantico, VA: US Marine Corps Studies and Analysis Division.

Grau, Lester W. and Timothy L. Thomas. 2000. Russian Lessons Learned From the Battles For Grozny. *Marine Corps Gazette*. Vol. 84, no. 4, April 2000: 45-48.

Grau, Lester W. and Timothy L. Thomas. 2000. Soft Log And Concrete Canyons: Russian Urban Combat Logistics In Grozny. In *The City's Many Faces:*

Proceedings of the RAND Arroyo-MCWL-J8 UWG Urban Operations Conference held in Washington, DC 13-14 April 1999, edited by Russell W. Glenn, 633-649, Santa Monica, CA: Rand.

Heggoy, Alf Andrew. 1972. *Insurgency and Counterinsurgency in Algeria.* Bloomington, IN: Indiana University Press.

Horne, Alister. 1977. *A Savage War of Peace.* Middlesex, England: Penguin Books Ltd.

Kelly, Robert E. 2000. US Army Special Forces Unconventional Warfare Doctrine: Engine of Change or Relic of the Past? Final report, Naval War College.

Kohl, James, and John Litt. 1974. *Urban Guerrilla Warfare in Latin America.* Cambridge, MA: The MIT Press.

Kulikov, Anatoly Sergeevich. 2001. The First Battle Of Grozny. In *Capital Preservation, Preparing for Urban Operations in the Twenty-First Century: Proceedings of the RAND Arroyo-TRADOC-MCWL-OSD Urban Operations Conference held in Santa Monica, CA 22-23 March 2000,* edited by Russell W. Glenn, 13-57, Santa Monica, CA: Rand.

Mallin, Jay. 1971. *Terror and Urban Guerillas: A Study of Tactics and Documents.* Coral Gables, FL: University of Miami Press.

Marine Corps Intelligence Activity. 1999. *Urban Warfare Study: City Case Studies Compilation.* Quantico, VA: Marine Corps Intelligence Activity.

Molnar, Andrew R., Jerry M. Tinker, and John D. LeNoir. 1965. *Human Factors Considerations of Undergrounds in Insurgencies.* Washington, DC: US Government Printing Office.

Oliker, Olga. 2001. *Russia's Chechen Wars 1994-2000: Lessons from Urban Combat.* Santa Monica, CA: Rand.

Oppenheimer, Martin. 1969. *The Urban Guerrilla.* Chicago, IL: Quadrangle Books.

Porzecanski, Arturo C. 1973. *Uruguay's Tupamaros: The Urban Guerrilla.* New York, NY: Praeger Publishers.

Presentation of Anatoly Sergeevich Kulikov. 2002. A briefing given to students at the US Army Command and General Staff College. Fort Leavenworth, KS.

Russian General Staff. 2002. *The Soviet-Afghan War: How a Superpower Fought and Lost.* Translated and edited by Lester W. Grau and Michael A. Gress. Lawrence, KS: University Press of Kansas.

Speyer, Arthur L., III. 2001. The Two Sides Of Grozny. In *Capital Preservation, Preparing for Urban Operations in the Twenty-First Century: Proceedings of the RAND Arroyo-TRADOC-MCWL-OSD Urban Operations Conference held in Santa Monica, CA 22-23 March 2000,* edited by Russell W. Glenn, 59-97, Santa Monica, CA: Rand.

Spiller, Roger J. 2000. *Sharp Corners: Urban Operations at Century's End.* Fort Leavenworth, KS: US Army Command and General Staff College Press.

Taw, Jennifer M. and Bruce Hoffman. 1994. *The Urbanization of Insurgency: The Potential Challenge to US Army Operations.* Santa Monica, CA: Rand.

Thomas, Timothy L. 1995. The Caucus Conflict and Russian Security: The Russian Armed Forces Confront Chechnya - Part One, Section Two: Military Activities of the Conflict During 11-31 December 1994. *Slavic Military Studies* 8, no. 2 (June 1995): 257-290.

Thomas, Timothy L. 1995. The Caucus Conflict and Russian Security: The Russian Armed Forces Confront Chechnya - Part One, Section One: From Intervention to the Outskirts of Grozny (Military-Political Events from 11 December to 31 December). *Slavic Military Studies* 8, no. 2 (June 1995): 233-256.

Thomas, Timothy L. 1997. The Caucus Conflict and Russian Security: The Russian Armed Forces Confront Chechnya III: The Battle for Grozny, 1-26 January 1995. *Slavic Military Studies* 10, no. 1 (March 1997): 50-108.

Thomas, Timothy L. 1999. The Battle of Grozny: Deadly Classroom For Urban Combat. *Parameters.* Vol. 29, Summer 1999: 87-102.

Thomas, Timothy L. 2000. Grozny 2000: Urban Combat Lessons Learned. *Military Review* LXXX, no. 4 (July-August): 50-58.

US Army. Command and General Staff College. 2002. *Student Text 27-1, Military Law.* Ft. Leavenworth, KS: USA CGSC, July.

White, Robert W. 1993. *Provisional Irish Republicans: An Oral and Interpretive History.* Westport, CT: Greenwood Press.

INITIAL DISTRIBUTION LIST

Combined Arms Research Library
US Army Command and General Staff College
250 Gibbon Ave.
Fort Leavenworth, KS 66027-2314

Defense Technical Information Center/OCA
825 John J. Kingman Rd., Suite 944
Fort Belvoir, VA 22060-6218

LTC Taylor V. Beattie
Department of Joint and Multinational Operations
USACGSC
1 Reynolds Ave.
Fort Leavenworth, KS 66027-1352

Dr. James H. Willbanks
Department of Joint and Multinational Operations
USACGSC
1 Reynolds Ave.
Fort Leavenworth, KS 66027-1352

MAJ Susan E. Mitchell
Military Law Office
USACGSC
1 Reynolds Ave.
Fort Leavenworth, KS 66027-1352

CERTIFICATION FOR MMAS DISTRIBUTION STATEMENT

1. Certification Date: 6 June 2003

2. Thesis Author: Patrick D. Marques

3. Thesis Title: Guerrilla Warfare Tactics In Urban Environments

4. Thesis Committee Members: LTC Taylor V. Beattie_____

   Signatures: Dr. James H. Willbanks_____

                                  MAJ Susan E. Mitchell_____

5. Distribution Statement: See distribution statements A-X on reverse, then circle appropriate distribution statement letter code below:

(A) B   C   D   E   F   X   SEE EXPLANATION OF CODES ON REVERSE

If your thesis does not fit into any of the above categories or is classified, you must coordinate with the classified section at CARL.

6. Justification: Justification is required for any distribution other than described in Distribution Statement A. All or part of a thesis may justify distribution limitation. See limitation justification statements 1-10 on reverse, then list, below, the statement(s) that applies (apply) to your thesis and corresponding chapters/sections and pages. Follow sample format shown below:

EXAMPLE

Limitation Justification Statement	/	Chapter/Section	/	Page(s)
Direct Military Support (10)	/	Chapter 3	/	12
Critical Technology (3)	/	Section 4	/	31
Administrative Operational Use (7)	/	Chapter 2	/	13-32

Fill in limitation justification for your thesis below:

Limitation Justification Statement	/	Chapter/Section	/	Page(s)
_____	/	_____	/	_____
_____	/	_____	/	_____
_____	/	_____	/	_____
_____	/	_____	/	_____
_____	/	_____	/	_____

7. MMAS Thesis Author's Signature: _____

STATEMENT A: Approved for public release; distribution is unlimited. (Documents with this statement may be made available or sold to the general public and foreign nationals).

STATEMENT B: Distribution authorized to US Government agencies only (insert reason and date ON REVERSE OF THIS FORM). Currently used reasons for imposing this statement include the following:

    1. Foreign Government Information. Protection of foreign information.

    2. Proprietary Information. Protection of proprietary information not owned by the US Government.

    3. Critical Technology. Protection and control of critical technology including technical data with potential military application.

    4. Test and Evaluation. Protection of test and evaluation of commercial production or military hardware.

    5. Contractor Performance Evaluation. Protection of information involving contractor performance evaluation.

    6. Premature Dissemination. Protection of information involving systems or hardware from premature dissemination.

    7. Administrative/Operational Use. Protection of information restricted to official use or for administrative or operational purposes.

    8. Software Documentation. Protection of software documentation - release only in accordance with the provisions of DoD Instruction 7930.2.

    9. Specific Authority. Protection of information required by a specific authority.

    10. Direct Military Support. To protect export-controlled technical data of such military significance that release for purposes other than direct support of DoD-approved activities may jeopardize a US military advantage.

STATEMENT C: Distribution authorized to US Government agencies and their contractors: (REASON AND DATE). Currently most used reasons are 1, 3, 7, 8, and 9 above.

STATEMENT D: Distribution authorized to DoD and US DoD contractors only; (REASON AND DATE). Currently most reasons are 1, 3, 7, 8, and 9 above.

STATEMENT E: Distribution authorized to DoD only; (REASON AND DATE). Currently most used reasons are 1, 2, 3, 4, 5, 6, 7, 8, 9, and 10.

STATEMENT F: Further dissemination only as directed by (controlling DoD office and date), or higher DoD authority. Used when the DoD originator determines that information is subject to special dissemination limitation specified by paragraph 4-505, DoD 5200.1-R.

STATEMENT X: Distribution authorized to US Government agencies and private individuals of enterprises eligible to obtain export-controlled technical data in accordance with DoD Directive 5230.25; (date). Controlling DoD office is (insert).

Back Exercise

STABILIZE, MOBILIZE, AND REDUCE PAIN

Brian Richey

**HUMAN
KINETICS**

Library of Congress Cataloging-in-Publication Data

Names: Richey, Brian, 1971- author.
Title: Back exercise : stabilize, mobilize, and reduce pain / Brian Richey.
Description: Champaign, IL : Human Kinetics, [2021] | Includes
  bibliographical references and index.
Identifiers: LCCN 2020030764 (print) | LCCN 2020030765 (ebook) | ISBN
  9781492594765 (paperback) | ISBN 9781492594772 (epub) | ISBN
  9781492594789 (pdf)
Subjects: LCSH: Backache--Exercise therapy. | Backache--Treatment.
Classification: LCC RD771.B217 R54 2021 (print) | LCC RD771.B217 (ebook)
  | DDC 617.5/64--dc23
LC record available at https://lccn.loc.gov/2020030764
LC ebook record available at https://lccn.loc.gov/2020030765

ISBN: 978-1-4925-9476-5 (print)

Senior Acquisitions Editor: Michelle Maloney; **Developmental Editor:** Laura Pulliam; **Managing Editor:** Miranda K. Baur; **Copyeditor:** Lisa Himes; **Indexer:** Nancy Ball; **Permissions Manager:** Martha Gullo; **Senior Graphic Designer:** Sean Roosevelt; **Cover Designer:** Keri Evans; **Cover Design Specialist:** Susan Rothermel Allen; **Photograph (cover):** © Balanced Body, Inc. Used with kind permission; **Photographs (interior):** Clay model images printed on pages 10, 11, and 15 © Balanced Body, Inc. Used with kind permission. All other photographs are © Human Kinetics; **Photo Production Specialist:** Amy Rose; **Photo Production Manager:** Jason Allen; **Senior Art Manager:** Kelly Hendren; **Illustrations:** © Human Kinetics; **Printer:** Sheridan Books

We thank Fit 4 Life DC in Washington, D.C., for assistance in providing the location for the photo shoot for this book.

Human Kinetics books are available at special discounts for bulk purchase. Special editions or book excerpts can also be created to specification. For details, contact the Special Sales Manager at Human Kinetics.

Printed in the United States of America   10 9 8 7 6 5 4 3 2 1

The paper in this book is certified under a sustainable forestry program.

Human Kinetics
1607 N. Market Street
Champaign, IL 61820
USA

United States and International
Website: **US.HumanKinetics.com**
Email: info@hkusa.com
Phone: 1-800-747-4457

Canada
Website: **Canada.HumanKinetics.com**
Email: info@hkcanada.com

E7993

Tell us what you think!
Human Kinetics would love to hear what we can do to improve the customer experience. Use this QR code to take our brief survey.